# The Treasure of Captain Claw

For Grace – J.E.

For Angela – S.C.

ORCHARD BOOKS
338 Euston Road, London NW1 3BH
*Orchard Books Australia*
Level 17/207 Kent Street, Sydney, NSW 2000

First published in 2011 by Orchard Books
First published in paperback in 2012

Text © Jonathan Emmett 2011
Illustrations © Steve Cox 2011

ISBN 978 1 84616 741 6

A CIP catalogue record for this book is available from the British Library.

1 3 5 7 9 10 8 6 4 2

Printed in China

Orchard Books is a division of Hachette Children's Books,
an Hachette UK company.

www.hachette.co.uk

You can find out more about Jonathan Emmett's books at
www.scribblestreet.co.uk

# The Treasure of Captain Claw

Jonathan Emmett

Steve Cox

ORCHARD

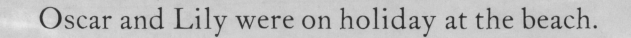

Oscar and Lily were on holiday at the beach.

Oscar was just starting his first triple-fudge sundae of the morning, while Lily was just finishing her fourth, when a jar washed up on the beach beside them.

"Treacle toffee!" said Oscar, reading the faded label. "My favourite!" said Lily, wiping her mouth.

It was a very old jar and very hard to open and Lily was disappointed to find that there was no toffee inside. But there was . . .

. . . a map!
The map showed an island with a big red cross.

"Treasure!" said Lily excitedly.

"I bet it's somewhere around here," said Oscar.

They packed some snacks for the journey
and set off in search of the treasure.

They hadn't gone far before Lily was hungry.
So they landed on a small shady island for a
mid-morning picnic.

One snack led to another and it wasn't long before all that was left was a dollop of stinky cheese that had gone off in the sun.

They didn't want to leave litter on the island, but the cheese was INCREDIBLY stinky. So Lily buried it in a hamper and Oscar drew a map so they could pick it up on their way home.

They set off once more, but it wasn't long before they were lost.

"Can you see any sign of land?" asked Oscar, checking the treasure map.

"I can't see anything at all," said Lily, looking around.

But something
could see them . . .

It was a
# PIRATE SUBMARINE!

"What do you want with us?"
demanded Oscar.
"When are you going to feed us?"
demanded Lily.
They were taken to the captain's
cabin and locked inside.

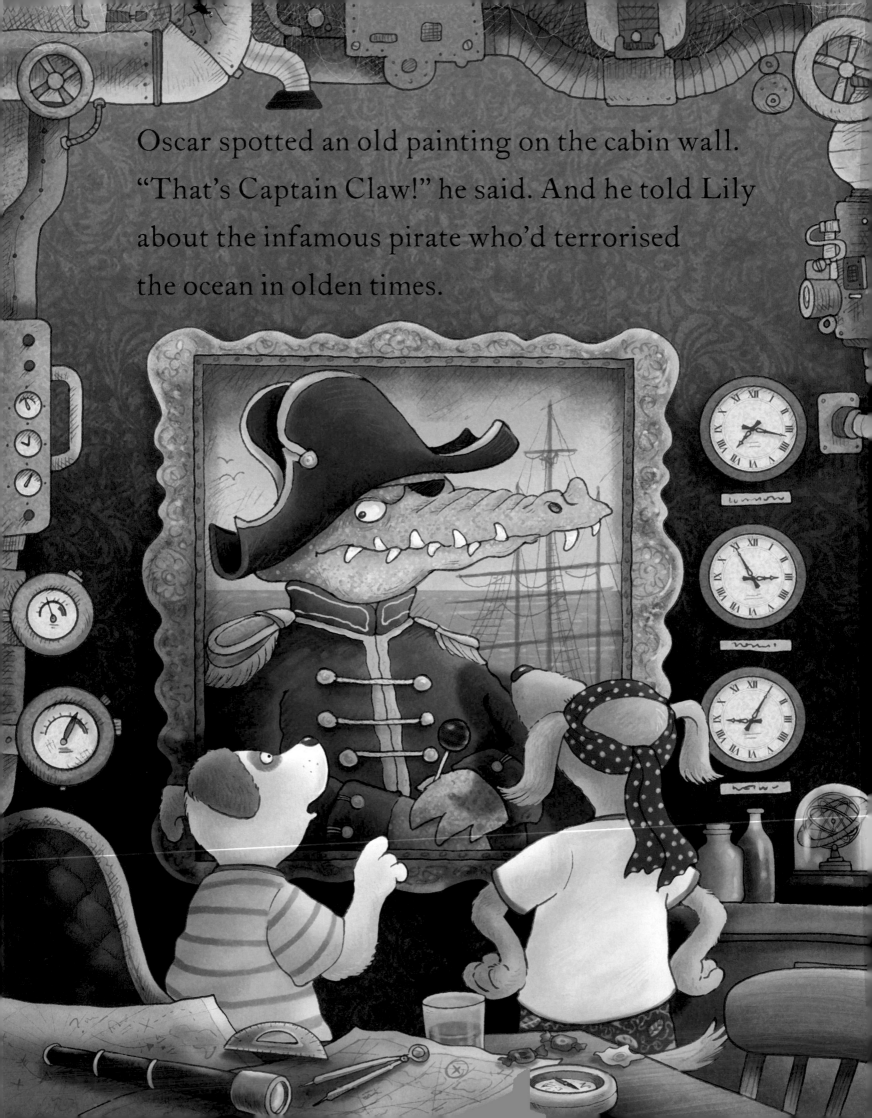

Oscar spotted an old painting on the cabin wall. "That's Captain Claw!" he said. And he told Lily about the infamous pirate who'd terrorised the ocean in olden times.

1 Provisions store
2 Loading bay
3 Escape hatch
4 Observation platform
5 Buoyancy tanks
6 Reserve power supply
7 Bridge
8 Galley and mess
9 Conning tower
10 Mini-sub docking bay
11 Communications centre

12 Control room
13 Secret treasure stash
14 Captain Claw's cabin
15 Fuel tanks
16 Waste disposal system
17 Crew's quarters
18 Engine room

Oscar and Lily were captured
and taken on board.

"It must be his treasure map we found!" Oscar realised.
They were so busy looking at the painting,
they didn't notice someone enter the cabin …

"It's him!" gasped Lily. "It's Captain Claw!"

"Captain Claw the Fifth, actually," said the crocodile.
"I'm his great-great-grandson. I've spent my whole life
searching for that treasure – so give me the map."

"No!" said Oscar.

"Not unless you give us some dinner first,"
added Lily hopefully.

"Give me the map –
or you'll BE the dinner!"
snarled Captain Claw.

Suddenly Lily didn't feel hungry any more.
"There's no need to snap," said Oscar, handing over the map.

Captain Claw took the submarine to a nearby island . . .

. . . and kicked Oscar and Lily out.

They climbed to the top of a hill
to find out where they were.

"If only we had a map!"
sighed Lily . . .

"Like this one?" said Oscar,
pulling the treasure map
out of his pocket.

Lily looked at the map. The island looked just like the one they were standing on. "But that means . . ." she gasped.

Oscar nodded. ". . . that the treasure is buried RIGHT HERE!"

They soon found a treasure chest full of shiny coins.
"It's gold!" said Oscar excitedly.

"It's better than gold," said Lily,
peeling a layer of foil from one of the coins,
"it's CHOCOLATE!"

Soon Oscar and Lily were
on their way home.
"But if this is the
treasure map," said Lily,
"what did you give
to the pirates?"

On a small shady island, Captain Claw the Fifth
and his crew had just discovered something.

"Faster, you dogs, faster," shouted the treasure-hungry captain, as they heaved a box out of the sand.

"What's that dreadful stink?" muttered one of the pirates.
"It smells just like . . .

...STINKY CHEESE!"